Bruno

EYES AND EARS

PHOTO AND ART CREDITS
Permission to use the following photographs and illustrations is gratefully acknowledged:
pages 4 (top), 6, 7, 8, and 14, © by Howard Sochurek, Inc.; pages 4 (bottom) and 22, RDF/Visuals Unlimited;
pages 9, 11, 16, 18, 20 and 25, © 2003 by Patricia Tobin; page 13, © by Prof. P. Motta, SPL, Photo Researchers, Inc.;
page 17, A. L. Blum/Visuals Unlimited; pages 19 and 21, © 1998 by IllusionWorks, L.L.C. All rights reserved;
pages 23 and 24, L. Bassett/Visuals Unlimited; page 27, Fred Hossler/Visuals Unlimited;
page 28, John D. Cunningham/Visuals Unlimited; page 31, Jack Star/PhotoLink/PhotoDisc;
page 32, © by S. Camazine, Photo Researchers, Inc.

Library of Congress Cataloging-in-Publication Data
Simon, Seymour.
Eyes and ears / Seymour Simon.
p.   cm.
Summary: Describes the anatomy of the eye and ear, how those organs function
and some ways in which they may malfunction, and how the brain
is also involved in our seeing and hearing.
ISBN 0-688-15303-8 — ISBN 0-688-15304-6 (lib. bdg.)
1. Eye—Juvenile literature.   2. Ear—Juvenile literature.   [1. Eye.   2. Ear.   3. Vision.
4. Hearing.   5. Senses and sensation.]   I. Title.
QP475.7 .S553   2003
612.8'4—dc21   2002019060

2   3   4   5   6   7   8   9   10
❖
First Edition

To my grandchildren,
who have opened up my eyes and ears once again

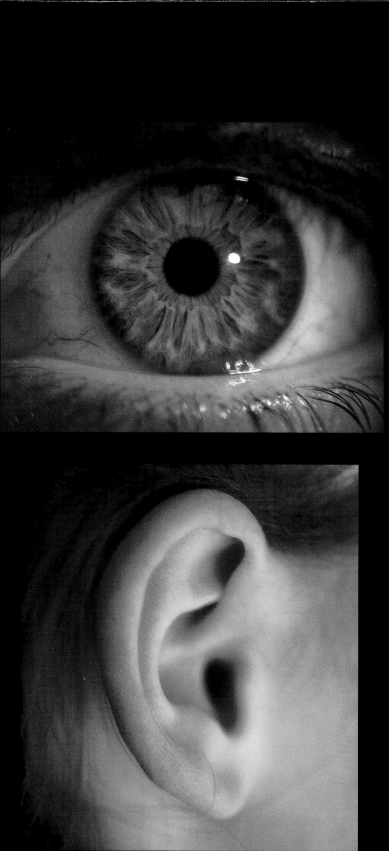

Light travels from objects and passes into our eyes. Light comes from many different sources, including the sun and electric bulbs. When light hits an object, light waves bounce off in all directions. Special light-sensitive cells in our eyes sense the light and send signals to our brain.

Sound waves move through the air and enter our ears. Sound is made when objects move back and forth, or vibrate. The vibrations travel through the air in invisible ripples called sound waves. Sound-sensitive cells in our ears sense the vibrations and send signals to our brain.

We see and hear when our brain makes sense out of the messages it gets from our eyes and our ears.

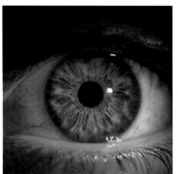

Your eye is also called an eyeball. It is shaped like a small ball about one inch across. Two eyeballs sit in cuplike sockets in the front of your head. Your eyelids cover parts of your eyes and make them appear more oval than round.

Six tiny muscles hold each eyeball steady in the sockets of your head. The muscles work in teams. One team of muscles swivels the eye toward or away from your nose. Another team of muscles moves the eye upward or downward. Still another team moves the eye at an angle down and outward or up and outward.

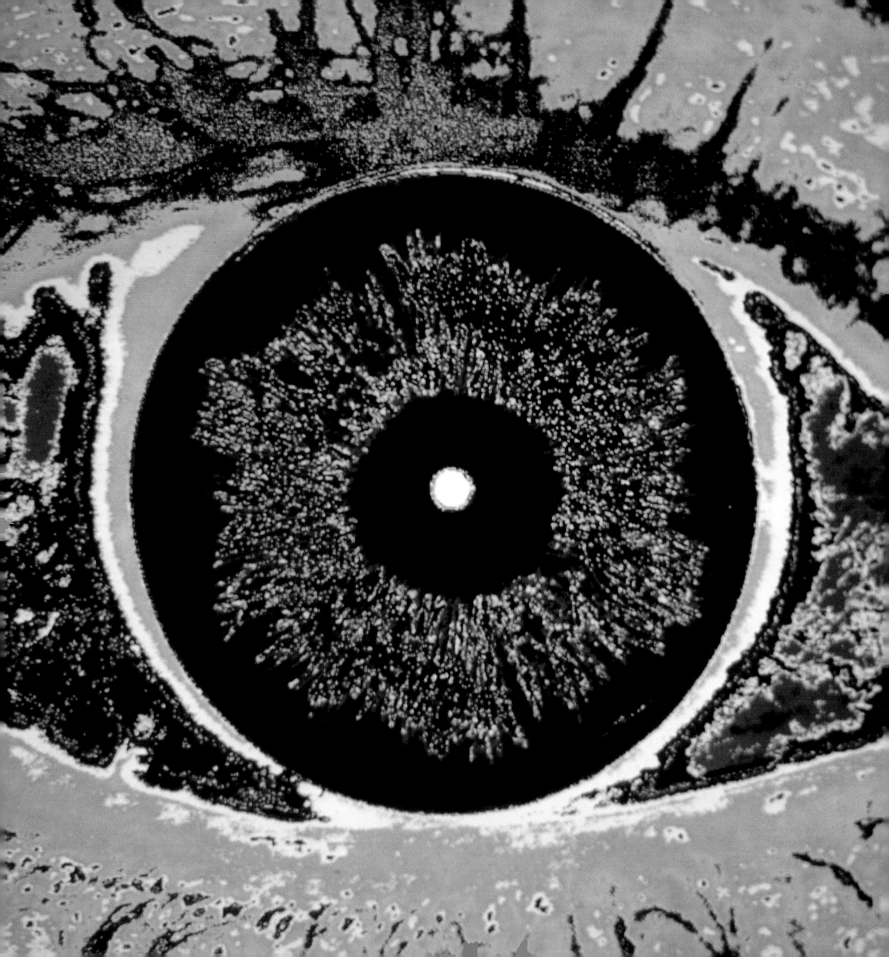

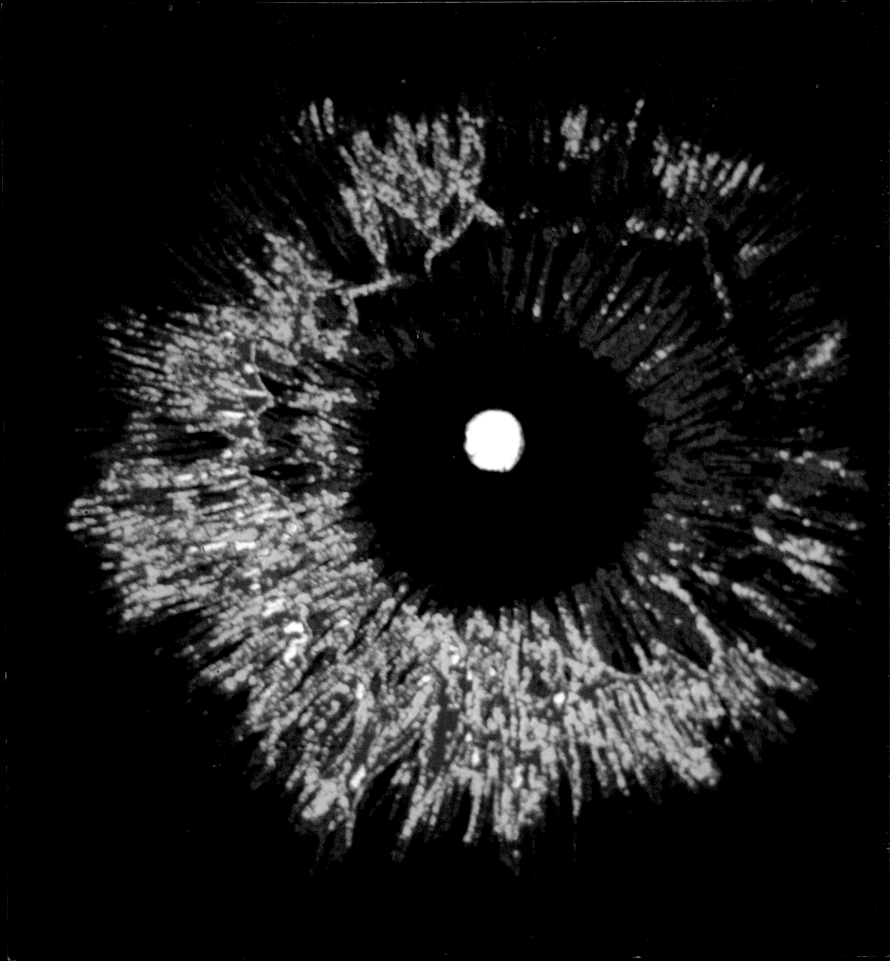

Rays of light enter the eyeball through a clear, round layer of cells called the cornea. The cornea acts like a camera lens and bends light into the eye.

The colored part of your eye just behind the cornea is called the iris. What color are *your* eyes? The opening in the central part of the iris is called the pupil. The size of the pupil is controlled by the muscles in the iris. The muscles tighten to make the pupil smaller in bright light and relax to make the pupil larger in dim light.

Light goes through the pupil and passes into the eye through the aqueous humor and then through the eye lens. The center of the eyeball contains a fluid called the vitreous humor. The vitreous humor fills the eyeball so that it has a rounded shape.

The lens focuses light through the vitreous humor onto the back of the eye, the retina. Light-sensitive cells in the retina are connected to the brain by a large optic nerve.

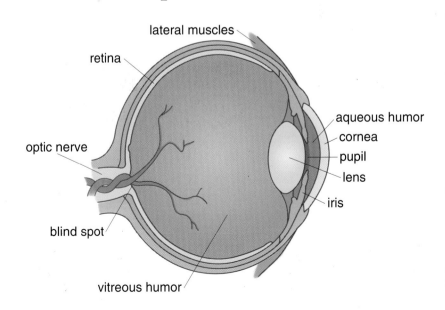

Here's what happens when you look at something, say a tree. Light reflected from the tree enters your eye through the pupil. The lens forms the light into an image that is a small picture of a tree. The image falls upside down on your retina.

In people with normal vision, light rays from an object are focused by the eye's lens exactly on the retina. But some people are nearsighted. They can see close objects clearly, but distant objects look blurred.

The reason for nearsightedness is that the eyeball in some people is a bit too long, front to back. Light rays from a distant object form an image in front of the retina. Nearsightedness, also called myopia, is corrected by wearing eyeglasses or contact lenses. The lenses change the focal point so that the image falls exactly on the retina.

Farsighted people see distant objects clearly, but closer objects look blurred. The eyeball is shorter front to back, so the image cannot be formed within the eye. Farsightedness, also called hyperopia, is corrected with differently shaped lenses in eyeglasses and contacts.

normal focus

nearsighted focus
(myopia)

farsighted focus
(hyperopia)

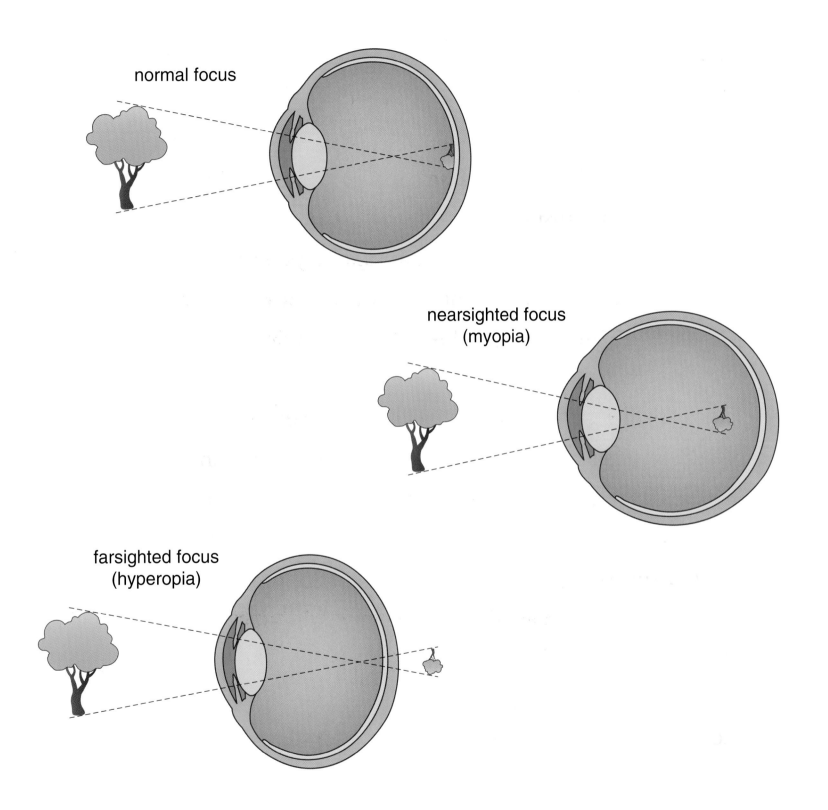

The retina contains two different kinds of light-sensitive nerve cells: rods and cones. They get their names because of the way they are shaped. Rod cells are sensitive to shades of brightness and are used to see in black and white. There are over one hundred million rod cells.

Cone cells work best in bright light and let us see color. There are about seven million cone cells in your retina. A tiny spot in the center of your eye contains only cones. It gives you the sharpest image. Around the edges of the retina are fewer cones and more and more rods. We use the cones more during the day and the rods more during the night.

The cone cells appear blue, while the numerous rod cells appear pink and purple.

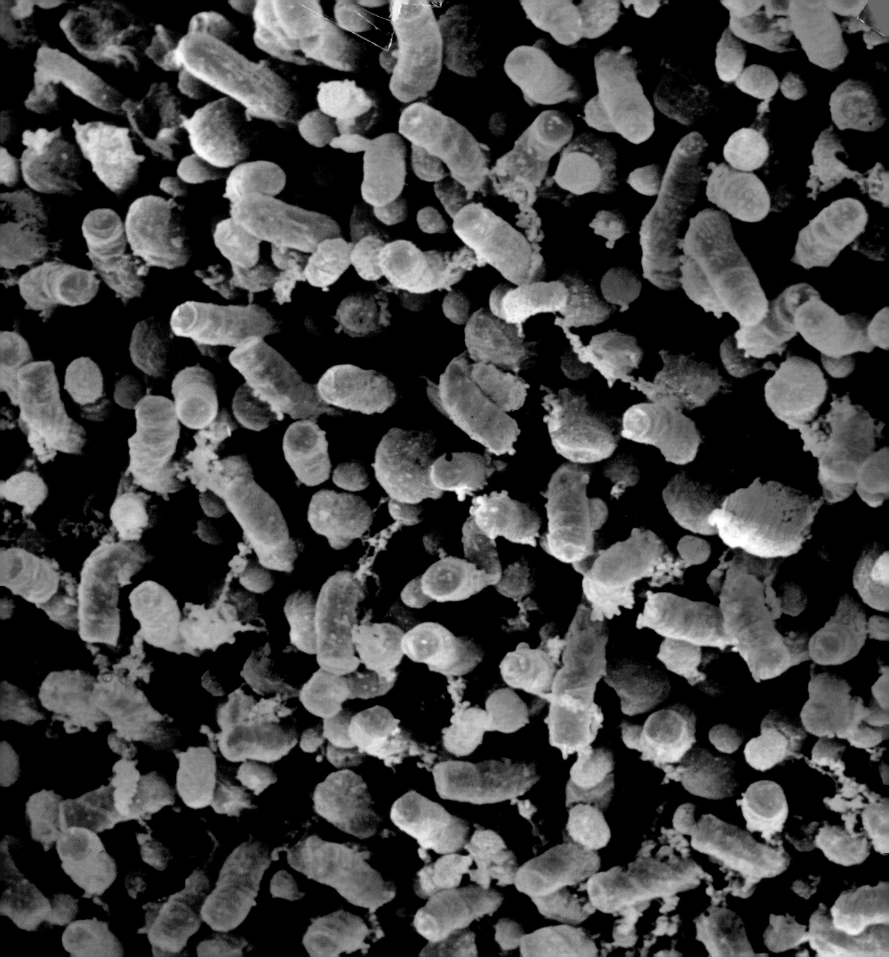

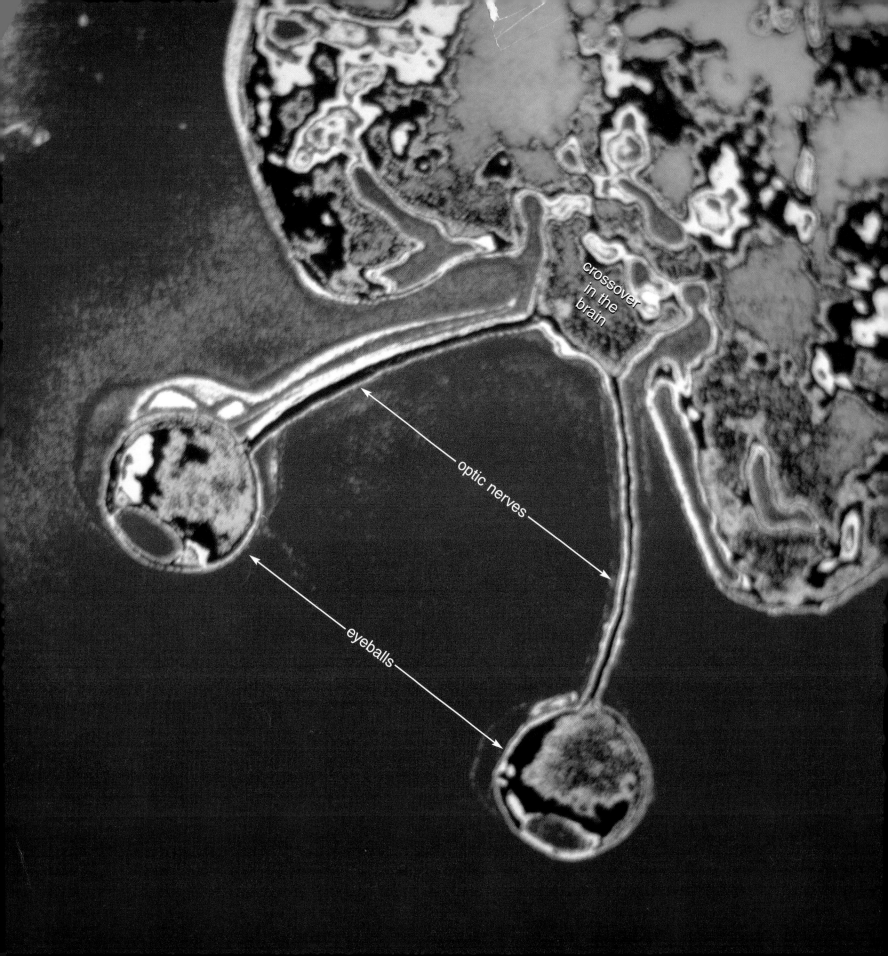

crossover
in the
brain

optic nerves

eyeballs

Every rod and cone cell in your retina is connected by its own nerve cell to the brain. When light strikes your retina, the cells respond. They send out tiny electric impulses. All the nerve cells collect at the back of the eye. They form a main cable called the optic nerve.

The optic nerve runs back from the eyeball through a tunnel in the skull to a crossover in the brain. The information from the right eye crosses over and goes to the left back of the brain. The information from the left eye crosses over and goes to the right back of the brain.

We still do not know exactly how the brain works. However, we do know that it is in your brain that seeing finally takes place. The brain puts together the nerve impulses from your eyes along with other brain impulses. The image is turned right side up, and you see what's out there.

There is one spot on the retina that is not sensitive to light. It is called the blind spot. It has no rods and cones because it is just at the point where the optic nerve goes out to the brain. Each of your eyes has its own blind spot (dark circle shown at right).

Usually you are not aware of the blind spots in your eyes. Your eyes are always moving around. You can get enough light images about what you are looking at so that you never notice the blind spot.

But here's a way of checking the blind spot in your right eye. Close your left eye and look at the X below with your right eye. Keep staring straight at the X while bringing the book closer to your eye. At about six to ten inches from your eye, you will no longer see the black dot to the side of the X. If you bring the book closer, the dot will appear again. At the point where you can't see the dot, the light from it falls just on the blind spot. If you want to check the blind spot in your left eye, turn the book over. Close your right eye and follow the same directions as above.

   •

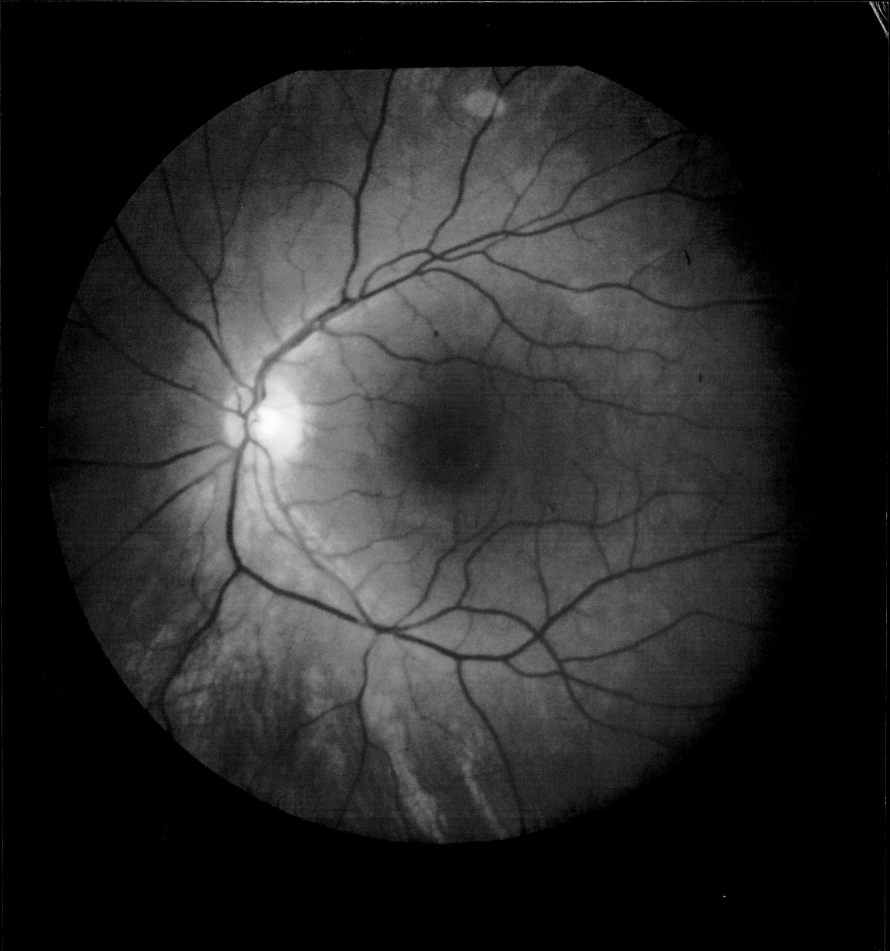

Sunlight is more than one hundred thousand times brighter than moonlight. That's why you can see colors in daylight but not in moonlight. The light of the moon looks silvery because you're seeing it with the color-blind rods in your retina. The color-sensing cones of your retina do not respond to the dim light of the moon.

As with everything else you see, your brain is involved in sensing color. Here's how you can show how your brain is involved in seeing color. Cut out a circle of white cardboard about four inches across. Color half green and the other half red. Push a two-inch nail through the center of the cardboard disk and trim the opening so that the disk spins freely on the nail. Spin it as rapidly as you can.

Your brain will combine the colors sensed by your eyes, and you will see a grayish tint instead of the green and red.

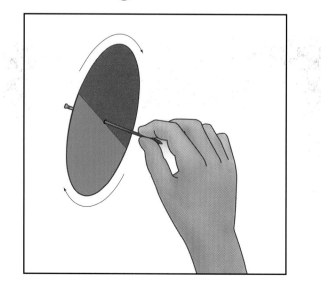

The colors you see are influenced by their surroundings. In the picture below, it looks as if the two crossing red lines are different colors, but they are both the same. The difference is that one has a background of white squares and the other a background of green squares.

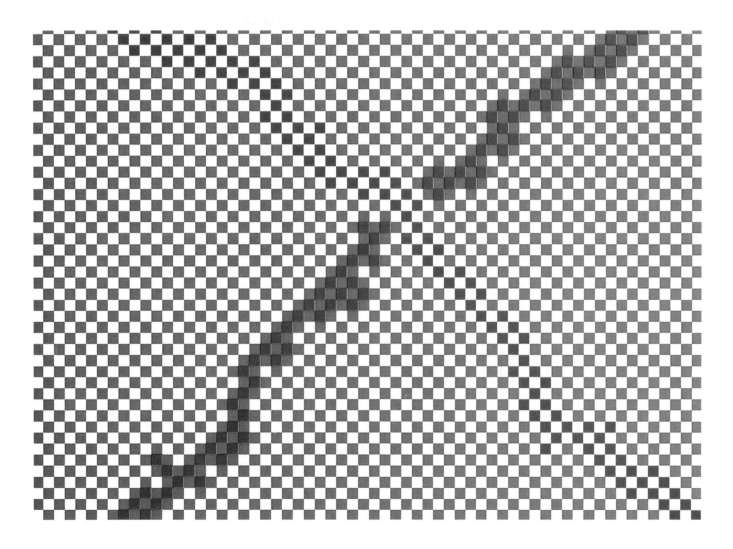

Sometimes you can't believe what your eyes and brain seem to see. An optical illusion is something that you think you see but is not exactly what is really there. Just to show you that everything you see is not so easy to figure out, look at the drawing below. It looks as if there are three prongs coming out at the right. But look to the left and see if you can figure out where the prongs come from. Try drawing the same figure on another sheet of paper. Even if you can draw it, you may not believe it!

There is another optical illusion on the opposite page. The dark lines in the painting look as if they are moving and pulsing, but they are really motionless. The colors in the painting are yellow and purple, but you may see other colors as well. Seeing all these colors is a trick of your mind and your eyes.

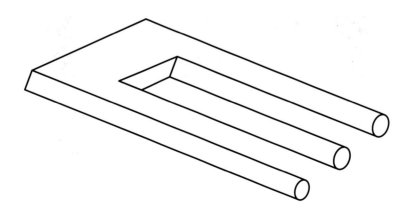

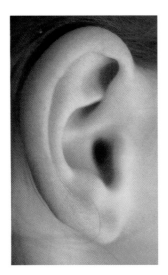

The ear is an amazing and important sense organ. We can hear all kinds of sounds, from the loud sound of a door slamming to the soft sound of tree leaves rustling in the wind. We can tell the sound of one friend's voice from that of another friend's voice. We use our ears to listen to radio and television and all of the everyday sounds around us.

An ear has three parts: the outer ear, the middle ear, and the inner ear. The earflaps on each side of your head are called pinnae. The pinnae are made of flexible cartilage and covered by a layer of skin. The bottom part of each pinna is called the earlobe. Some people have long and curved earlobes while others have small and flat earlobes.

The pinnae act as a kind of sound catcher. They channel the sound waves down a short tube called the auditory canal to the eardrum. The eardrum separates the outer ear from the middle ear.

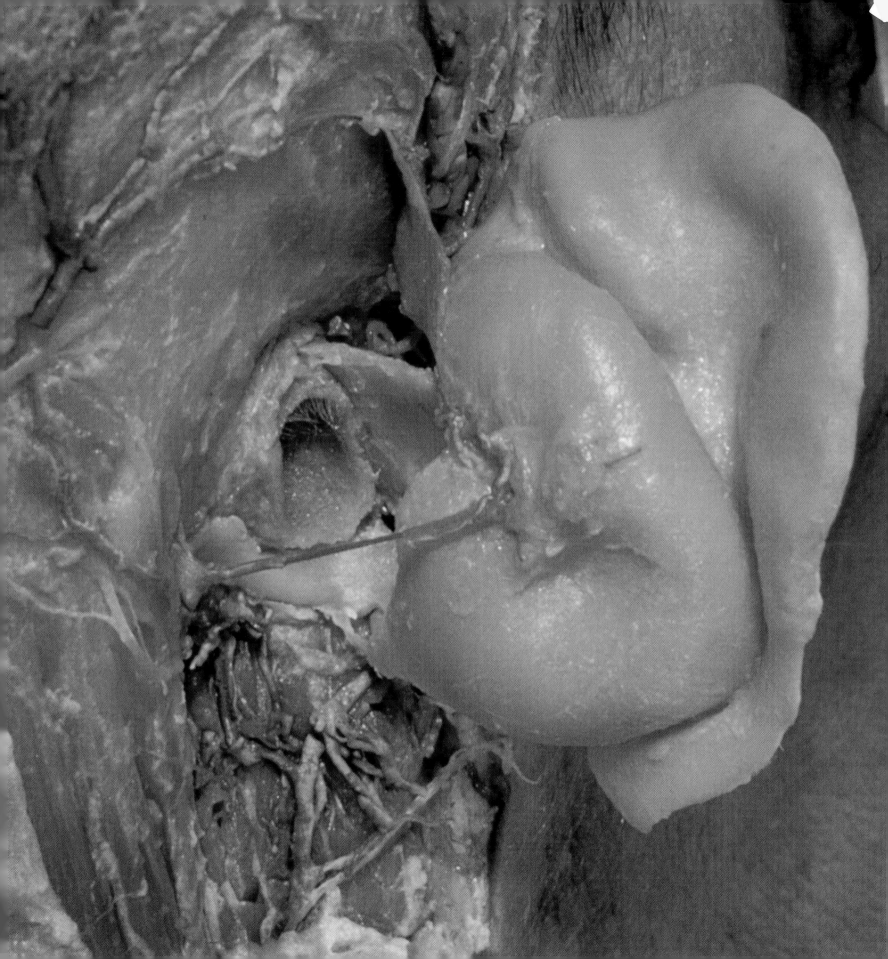

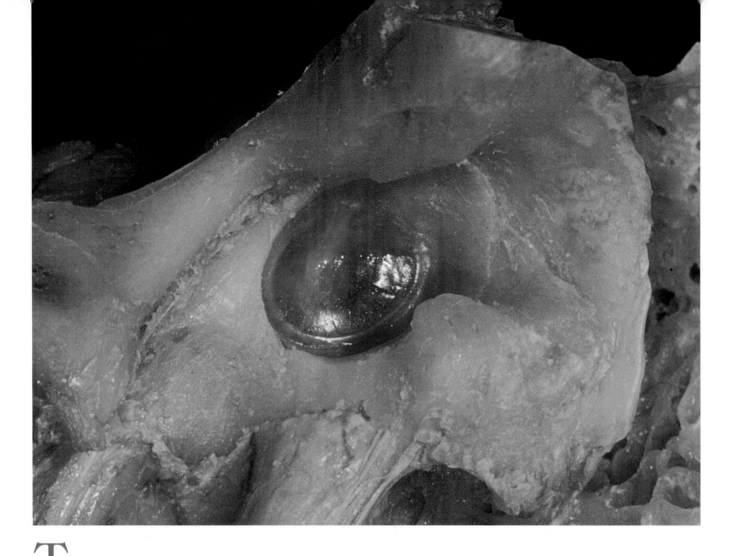

The eardrum is a thin flap of skin that stretches tightly across the end of the auditory canal. Sound waves cause the eardrum to vibrate just like the top of a drum when it is hit by a drumstick. The middle ear is a tiny space behind the eardrum.

Inside the middle ear are the three smallest bones in the body, linked together. They are called the hammer, the anvil, and the stirrup because of their shapes. These three bones together are also called the ossicles. The vibrations of the eardrum cause the ossicles to move. The movements are transmitted to another tight, thin flap of skin called the oval window.

The middle ear is linked to the back of your throat by the Eustachian tube. This narrow tube is usually closed. But when you swallow, chew, or yawn, the entrance to the tube opens and air travels in and out of your middle ear. That keeps the air pressure on either side of your eardrum the same. Sometimes your ears "pop" when the tubes suddenly open.

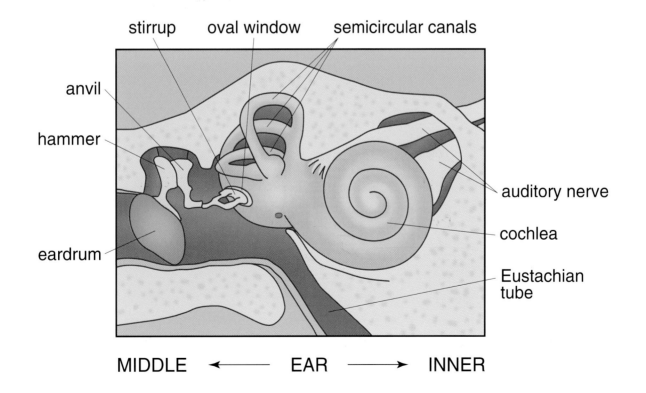

stirrup   oval window   semicircular canals

anvil

hammer

auditory nerve

cochlea

eardrum

Eustachian
tube

MIDDLE ←——— EAR ———→ INNER

Your inner ear lies in a bony hollow within your skull. The inner ear has a maze of spaces called the labyrinth. At the end of the labyrinth is a spiral, coiled tube shaped like a snail shell. It is called the cochlea from the Latin word for snail.

Inside the cochlea is a strip of skin covered with tiny hairs. The cochlea is filled with a fluid. When vibrations travel through the ear, they set off waves in the fluid. The waves cause the hairs to ripple like fields of grass in the wind.

At the bottom of each hair is a nerve cell. Each ear has about twenty thousand nerve cells. The cells send a message through the auditory nerve to the hearing centers in the brain. The brain tells you what the vibrations mean: your teacher talking, a car honking, or a paper rustling. Finally, you hear.

Nerve cells in a cochlea

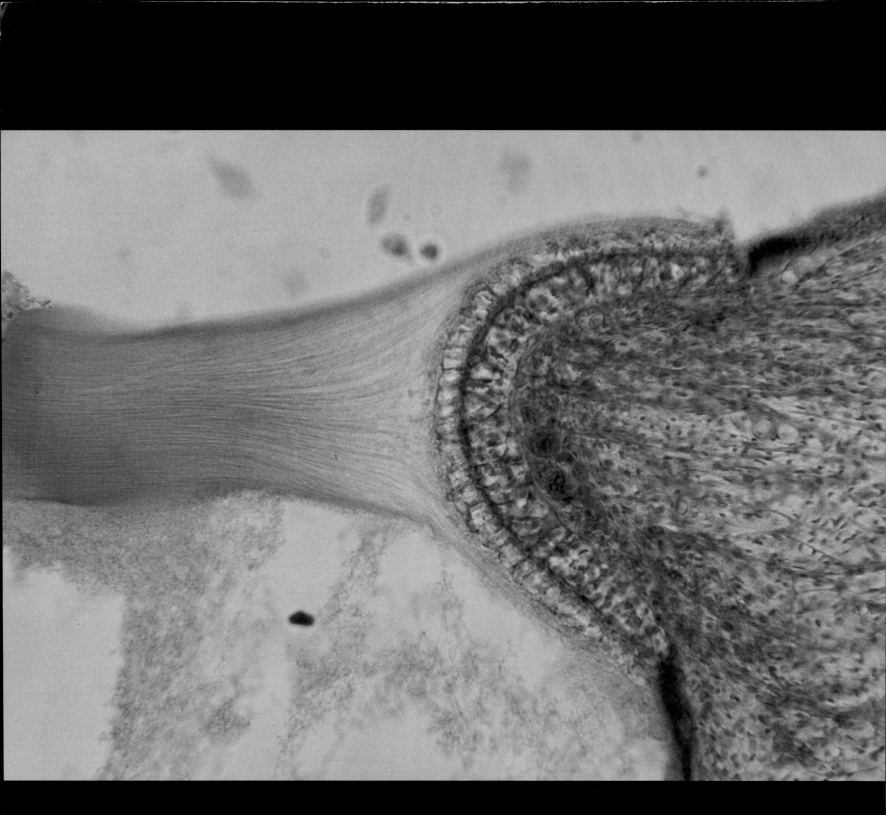

Nerve cells in a semicircular canal

The ears do another job. Next to the cochlea are three semicircular canals. These help you to keep your balance when you sit still, walk about, or jump and bend.

The curved tubes of the semicircular canals point in three directions. Like the cochlea, the canals are filled with a fluid and lined with a hairy skin. When you move your head in any direction, the fluid moves in at least one of the canals. Nerve cells in the canals send signals to the brain: You are moving up or down, to one side or another, backward or forward.

The signals let your brain know how you are moving and help keep you steady. Even with your eyes closed, you know the position of your head. However, if you whirl around and around, the fluid in the canals keeps moving for a few seconds even after you stop. Then you may get dizzy and lose your balance.

Some people may have difficulty hearing. Sometimes hearing loss is caused by a sticky material made inside the ears called earwax. Earwax can build up and collect dirt and dust. Then the outer ears have to be carefully cleaned to remove the blockage. You should never try to do this yourself because of the danger of hurting your eardrum.

As people get older, some will gradually become hard of hearing. They may use a hearing aid that fits inside their outer ear. Hearing aids make sounds louder to help people with this kind of deafness.

Some people are born with a severe hearing loss or lose their hearing as the result of an injury. They often use hearing aids as well as other machines to alert them to sounds. For example, special telephones can be made to flash a light instead of ringing a bell. Then the messages can be seen on a screen instead of being heard through an earpiece. Many hard-of-hearing people can understand what other people say by reading their lips.

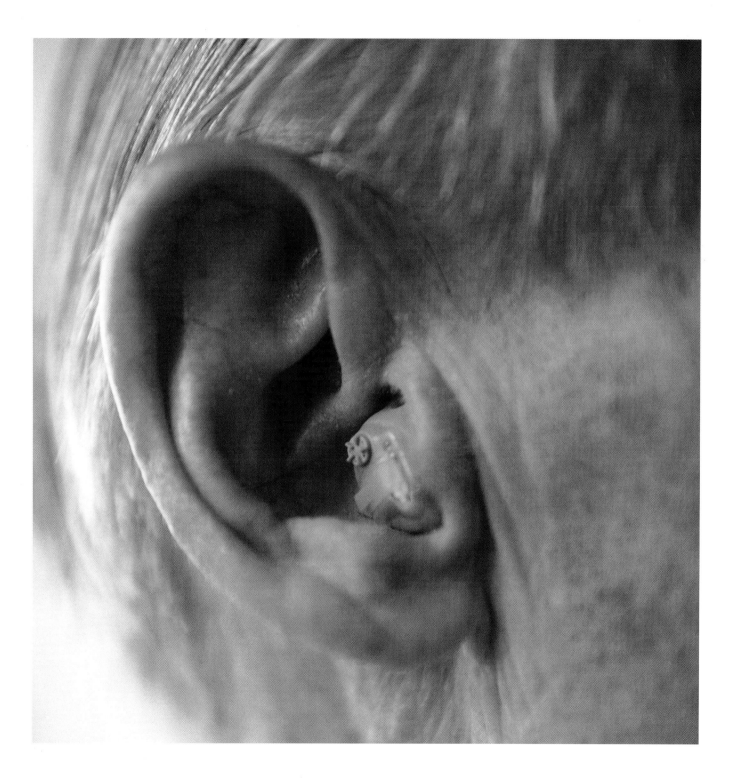

We use our senses to learn what is happening in the world around us. Our eyes and ears sense light and sound and send nerve signals to the brain. The brain puts the information together to let us see and hear.

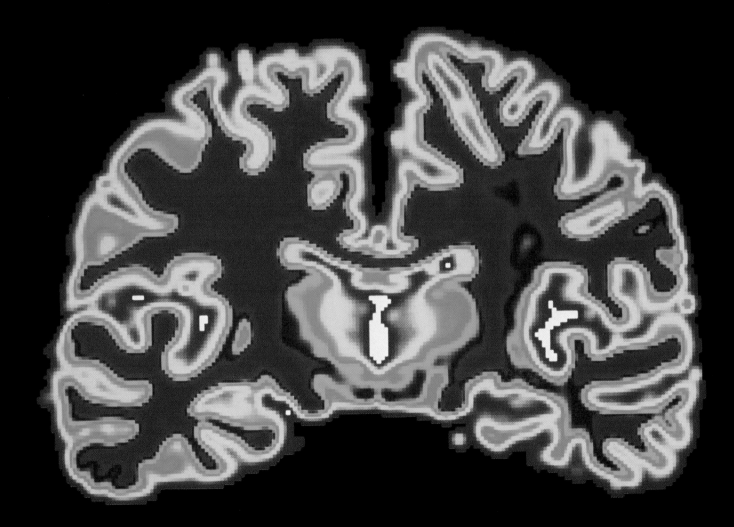